Conversations with
Papa Charlie

Conversations with
Papa Charlie

A Memory of Charles E. Smith

DAVID BRUCE SMITH

CAPITAL
BOOKS, INC.
Sterling, Virginia

Capital Books, Inc.
P.O. Box 605
Herndon, Virginia 20172-0605

ISBN 1-892123-34-7 (alk. paper)

Library of Congress Cataloging-in-Publication Data

Smith, David Bruce.
    Conversations with Papa Charlie : a memory of Charles E. Smith / by
David Bruce Smith.
        p. cm.
    ISBN 1-892123-34-7
    1. Smith, Charles E., 1901–   . 2. Construction industry—United States—
Biography. 3. Real estate developers—United States—Biography.
4. Businessmen—United States—Biography. 5. Philanthropists—United
States—Biography. I. Title.

    HC102.5.S43 S45 2000
    338.7′624′092—dc21
    [B]   00-057913

    Printed in Canada on acid-free paper that meets the American National
Standards Institute Z39-48 Standard.

    First Edition

    10   9   8   7   6   5   4   3   2   1

For Harriet,
and to my grandmother
Betty Siegel Chasen . . .

but especially for Liz

The commonest axiom of history is that every generation revolts against its fathers and makes friends with its grandfathers.
—*Lewis Mumford*, The Brown Decades

Contents

Acknowledgments

I want to thank so very much the people who helped and influenced this book either directly or indirectly.

My longtime friend Wendy Dubit has encouraged me for years, which is very much appreciated. She introduced me to Muriel Nellis, who became my literary agent. Muriel united me with the wonderfully talented Phil Trupp, who gave me hours of editorial advice and suggestions that have made this book much better than it would have been.

Thank you also to Marlena Brown-Tumlin and Sarah Pickeral; to Mom and Dad and my sister and brother, Michelle and Steven; to Ruth and Robert St. John, Peggy Heller, Lillian Brown, and Judy and Jerry Miller; to Merle Tabor Stern and Murray Bognovitz; to Amalia Corado, Carlos Lopes, and Jan Singleton for being so kind to my grandfather; to my special friends and coworkers Jane Lynch, Janet Meglen, Nick DiLella, and George Zagas; to wonderful Kelly Lynch, my assistant; and to Dr. William Stark, with love.

Prologue

At first I wanted to compose a thoroughly tentacled biography of my grandfather.

The book was not coalescing. Yet I was positive it was worthwhile. Besides knowing Papa Charlie intimately, I knew that his humor, wisdom, and enthusiasm for life contained memorable lessons, even for strangers. This concise format is appropriate and representative of my grandfather. He was impatient with verbosity and swollen prose.

I was a lucky grandson. Papa Charlie was kind and gentle, and his laughter could instantly dispel sadness. His eyes always sparkled with youth because he was ever youthful and adventurous. But the most important thing he did for me was to constantly encourage me, even if I didn't always understand why.

Papa Charlie's life had a singular rhythm: obstruction, conquer it; obstruction, push it aside.

His strong sense of responsibility started early. Charles E. Smith began his life March 28, 1901, in the Russian village of Lipnick in a hilly, rural region near the Don and Volga Rivers. He emigrated to America in September 1911. By the time he was in his middle twenties he had become a successful builder of homes and strip centers in Brooklyn. He lost almost everything in the Great Depression and spent twenty years reconstructing his financial success by starting a second career as a builder of apartments, and later office buildings, in Washington, DC, Maryland, and Virginia.

That he was even alive my grandfather considered nothing less than a miracle. When he was seven he and two of his brothers, Chaim and Beryl, contracted diphtheria, for which there was no treatment. While my great-grandmother Sadie sat vigilantly at their bedsides, waiting for her sons to die, Papa Charlie suddenly screamed for water. He drank twelve glasses of warm liquid mixed with milk. The next morning he recovered, but Beryl and Chaim slept to their deaths. Papa Charlie attributed his survival to a "message from God," and the message was: He was destined to live and to do good works.

Similar communications appeared throughout Papa Charlie's life in chameleon forms: dreams, signs, or events that he interpreted as having significant meaning. They were powerful; they guided him into making some of his most important life decisions—the correct ones.

Fifty years later I was born two months prematurely in Washington, DC, weighing three and one-half pounds, with lungs that were obstructed by phlegm. The prognostications for my survival were as remote as they had been for Papa Charlie when he had diphtheria. Days passed without success in relieving my strained breathing. The doctors warned my parents that I might die. But Papa Charlie, who visited the hospital every day to see me, insisted they were wrong. He believed God would save me, as he had been spared, because he saw "fire in my eyes" and a desperate struggle to live.

Because of that nearly tragic circumstance we became immediately and inextricably involved by survival, blood, and a common near-death experience. As he had coughed up his diphtheria membrane two generations earlier, I would miraculously vomit my phlegm into two buckets, clearing the way for my life to begin.

"I have looked after you every single day of your life, and when I get to the Other Side, I will look after you every single day for the rest of your life—and don't ever forget it," he told me years later.

I may have been the writer of this book, but the words and the inspiration are mostly his.

One

"Papa Abby"

*Y*ou could say that Papa Charlie was sometimes my arbitrator and crisis cruncher, particularly when I was experiencing separation anxiety. With this issue I was not an easy child. When it came to parting from my family for long periods of time, I had enough tears to rust the Eiffel Tower.

My parents, my grandfather, and I were in Rome one summer, vacationing—well, at least they were. Although I was supposed to be enjoying the splendors of the Vatican, the Coliseum, and the delightful Italian food, I had no appetite for any of it. My stomach had a knot inside it the size of the Roman Empire. I was filled with dread about a trip I was to take when we returned home, a journey that would take me away from my parents for many weeks.

Because Papa Charlie and I were roommates at the splendid Grand Hotel, we had a lot of time to talk. He always knew when something was out of kilter with me.

"What is it?" he asked gently.

"I have to go on a four-week teen tour out West right after we get home."

"I see. Can you separate the two? Can you put that trip out of your mind for now and just enjoy this trip?"

"I can't. It feels like being sent to camp all over again. And you remember how that was for me, don't you?"

His face became very serious. "Not many nine-year-old boys call their summer camp 'Auschwitz.'"

"What should I do?" I pleaded.

"Talk to your dad."

"He'll get mad."

"No."

"Yes."

"He loves you, my David."

"I know that, Papa Charlie. But do you know how many times they've heard me complain and cry about leaving home? My mother and father don't want to hear me whine to them about being homesick at age four-teen—again."

"What if all of us talk about this tomorrow?" he suggested.

"Won't work." I had already begged them to let me out of it. The prospect of another discussion made me as anxious as the dreaded tour.

Papa Charlie rose from his bed and paced around the room, then turned and faced me. He was somber, as if he were listening to those inner voices that helped him guide such decisions.

"I don't think you're ready for it," he said at last.

"For what?"

"The trip. I'm going to talk to your dad myself tomorrow and see what he says."

Later I asked, "Was he disappointed?"

"I explained everything. Your father says it's your choice whether or not to go. I told him you weren't ready for it. I told them if they force you to go, you might resent them unnecessarily for years to come. The only thing your dad asks is that you make the telephone call if you choose to cancel."

I could feel my Roman-sized knot unraveling. "That's fair. What do you think I should do?"

"My David, I know your decision, and I support it *one thousand* percent. Now, please, enjoy the rest of this trip and the summer too."

Maybe he wasn't "Dear Abby," but he came close.

Two

Like Yourself Too

$\mathcal{B}$efore EST, *I'm OK, You're OK*, and a plethora of other how-to books and therapies, Papa Charlie was already a believer in liking himself and *talking* about it. He did not believe a person should be self-indulgent. But it was prudent, he felt, to be confident. Such an outlook allowed one to satisfy one's responsibilities with a clear mind. Papa Charlie's obligations included business, charitable, and familial commitments; he was supporting his sister, Betty, other relatives, and friends.

He recommended daily exercise; a meatless-and-sugarless diet; eight to ten glasses of hot or cold water each day, "to purify your body"; and hot milk or home-made low-fat yogurt milkshakes to help with sleep. He practiced deep breathing and relaxation exercises. But without an assured self-image, the rudimentary parts of his advice framework would suffer.

Every night he hypnotized each part of his body. He began by saying, "Toes, relax." Then he moved upward: "Feet, relax. I go all the way up, slowly," he explained. "By the time I get to my head, I'm already asleep!"

He encouraged many people to do this. "Go to bed with a smile," he said. "Be positive. It's important to be good to yourself. After all, you're the only one you've got!"

Three

Deliverer of Misery

$\mathcal{P}$apa Charlie was raised on a potato-and-corn farm in Russia. The family lived in a modest dirt-floored house that was warmed by a wood-burning stove. He grew up in an era in which Jews were prohibited from owning property. My great-grandfather Reuven leased the farm from a benevolent man. But when the owner died, an anti-Semitic heir expelled the family from their home.

They scattered. Reuven relocated everyone, pell-mell, to Great-Grandmother Sadie's relatives in nearby Paritch while he sought another way to make a living.

Eventually, Reuven decided to purchase a windmill with his brother, Nachum, to produce flour. The operation was a success, but shortly after it was begun the windmill burned to the ground in the middle of the night. No culprit was ever discovered.

The usually stoic Reuven, now unsure and shaken, went to the village *Guten Yid*, or "wise Jew," for advice, a common thing to do because many Russians relied on mystics and "messengers."

The old man listened to his story and said, "Reuven, you've had two signs from heaven. Pack up and go to America."

In 1908 Reuven sailed to New York to learn the carpentry and building trades from his brother Max. Papa Charlie, meanwhile, at the age of seven, became the "little man" of the family, helping his mother manage the household until his father sent for them three years later.

When they arrived in New York, Papa Charlie noticed that Reuven had Americanized his appearance by replacing his rabbi-length beard with a Vandyke. He also now worked six days a week, including Saturday, the Jewish sabbath, to accommodate his new non-Jewish world.

Reuven had rented an apartment in a poor Jewish section of Brooklyn called Brownsville and settled the family into a three-bedroom, second-floor walk-up illuminated sparsely by gaslight. Papa Charlie's older cousins, Celia and Sophie Gorelick, who had jobs as milliners, also came to live with them.

"I was no different from the hundreds of other immigrants around me," Papa Charlie remembered. "But I had confidence that I would succeed by learning the language and making many friends—and I did."

Still, there were obstacles. Adjusting to a new country was not easy.

When Reuven took Papa Charlie to his first day at P.S. 125, the school officials gave him an oral examination, which luckily emphasized mathematics. Papa Charlie did not yet speak a word of English. But because math had always been his favorite subject, he received a high score and was placed in the fourth grade. Within a few months he advanced to his peer group—the sixth grade.

"I imagine my accent sounded very thick," he recalled. "When I would walk to school with my new friend, David Kravitz, a boy in my class would shout, 'Greenhorn!' I told David I was tired of being called that name. 'I'm going to ask him to stop, and if he doesn't, I'll have to fight him.'"

"Greenhorn!" the boy taunted Papa Charlie the next day.

"Please stop calling me 'Greenhorn'; I don't like it," Papa Charlie warned.

"Greenhorn! Greenhorn! *Greenhorn!*"

Papa Charlie put up his hands. "So I fought. I threw him to the ground and growled, 'Do you give up now?' "

He was not ridiculed again.

Papa Charlie never forgot this traumatic event. To fight for something. It evolved, perhaps, into a "sign" that carried him through the years.

"What does this fight impulse mean?" I asked.

He grinned wickedly. In this case it means, "You can't swap jokes with the deliverer of misery." Or to put it in more modern terms: "Don't snicker at bad luck. Rise above it, or it kicks you."

Four

Enticed by Bad Advice

$\mathcal{B}$y 1928 Papa Charlie was at the zenith of his first cycle of business success. As part of his daily routine he visited his stockbroker to monitor his investments, noticing eventually that the market was fluctuating more than normal. He was uneasy about this and had a premonition that something disastrous was going to happen.

"I had this feeling the market was going to drop terribly—a feeling in my bones," Papa Charlie said.

It was more than a random premonition; this was yet another "message."

One day at lunch he confided to his business partner and cousin, David, "I'm worried about these shifts in the market." He paused, and suddenly his brown eyes flashed with feeling. He straightened his back, and it looked as if his body were going to rise above the table. "Let's get out," he said.

"I don't think we have anything to worry about," David replied.

"Each day when I go to our broker, I see that the market keeps going up and down. I think this is a bad sign. It shows that a lot of people in this country are uneasy. Let's get out," he repeated.

"Charlie, you've got tomato juice in your veins. If you're unhappy, you sell. I intend to stay in."

Papa Charlie cashed in all of his stock and deposited the money in three different savings and loans in case one of them collapsed.

A short time later the partners met again.

"David, I still think things look bad. Let's sell all of our buildings and lay low. Our money can earn 4 percent. That would be enough to live on comfortably. When things improve we can start building again."

"Charlie, you're worrying about nothing."

"If you're still against it, then I want to sell my half of the business," Papa Charlie said.

"Why don't we compromise?" David suggested. "We'll stay in the business for one more year. We'll do a lot more building, and then we'll get out."

"Okay, I'll go along with it," Papa Charlie said reluctantly. This decision was against his instincts, but he chose to ignore them.

They immediately sped up their construction schedule. Then in October 1929 the stock market caved in. Papa Charlie lost everything he had except the money left in the three savings and loans.

Until the end of his life Papa Charlie would tell us, "Always follow your intuition. You know more than you think, and remember: It takes a long time to make a lot of money but only a second to lose it."

Five

I Will Never Push a Pencil

When he was twenty-two Papa Charlie became an accountant to please his father, but he thought it was a bore. Over time his dream of becoming a builder overwhelmed him, and he quit the job. It was a bold move, and he knew his father would not approve. But he had a single ambition: to work with his hands and quit pushing pencils.

One Saturday night in 1923, without Reuven's knowledge, Papa Charlie went to visit his cousin, Alex, who owned a delicatessen in Newark. He waited for all of the customers to leave and then made an offer.

"Alex, you have the money and I have the experience. Let's go into the building business."

"Charlie, what do you know about the building business? Do you think free meals grow in Brooklyn?"

"Listen, I know quite a bit already," Papa Charlie said excitedly. "I write all of the contracts for my father, and on Saturdays and Sundays I stay on the job and sell his homes. I have learned a lot in the past three years."

Reuven believed that the real estate business was cyclical and risky, and he perceived accounting to be a source of a steady income. But some inner voice compelled Papa Charlie to go against his father's wishes—a radical decision in his family's Orthodox Jewish household, where Reuven was the absolute patriarch.

"Okay," Alex said. "Next Saturday I will come to your house and talk to your father."

The following week Reuven protested. "I don't approve!" he told Papa Charlie. Then he softened. "But if this is what you want, then so be it. I'll help in whatever way I can. If you like, I'll even help oversee construction."

Alex was delighted to hear this news. "Charlie, you and I are now partners, so go ahead and buy some ground and build!"

Their first project was the construction of three houses in Brooklyn, which sold for $8,500 each. The total profit of the job was $7,500, which they divided equally.

Again, Papa Charlie's inner voice proved to be right.

He said, on the job and in life, "Pursue *your* dreams, not someone else's. And *never* give up!"

Six

Leah's War

*P*apa Charlie revered his mother, but he didn't always take her advice. She disliked Leah Goldstein of Yonkers, New York, but my grandfather married her on February 8, 1927, at the St. George Hotel in Brooklyn.

Leah was the youngest of four girls. When she met Papa Charlie at the luxurious Lakeview resort in New Jersey, she was reconciling herself to a just-terminated engagement. Papa Charlie saw her coming up the stairs and was so entranced by her beauty that he introduced himself and handed her his engraved card. They danced together the entire evening. This meeting was followed by a year-long courtship.

Their newlywed months were happy until my grandmother Leah suddenly became ill with a high fever.

"The doctors didn't know what was wrong with her.

And then—oh, my God!" His face crinkled in horror. "They made the diagnosis of diphtheria. I asked myself, How could this be? We have just started out; we have a whole life to live together."

Leah was admitted to the hospital. The fever spiraled and broke daily.

"Leah was in critical condition for about three weeks. They couldn't stabilize her," Papa Charlie told me. "She was in and out of a coma. Finally she recovered and was able to come home. Within months she was pregnant with our son, Bob."

As the years passed, Leah's general behavior seemed to mirror the ups and downs of that fever. At times she was moody, argumentative, and irrational. Sometimes she was so agitated that she needed to be left alone. When her horrendous moods passed she would be humorous, happier, and fun to be with.

We were not told of these episodes. I heard of them years later, mostly from Papa Charlie, who may have been relieved to discuss them.

"Were you happy with Nana?" I asked.

"Sometimes. But as you know, we had to separate a few years before her death."

"I remember. Why did you continue to see her so often and stick by her?"

His lips tightened. "I would not divorce her."

"That doesn't answer my question."

"I stayed on because . . ." His eyes started to tear. He reached into his pocket for a handkerchief. "I stayed on because I knew that when your grandmother was in one of her bad periods it was the illness speaking, not her." He paused, replaced the handkerchief in his right back pocket. "Leah was smart. A good woman. Honorable. She just couldn't help herself at times. When she became angry she was impossible and scary. She said mean things to our friends. Many times I had to apologize for her behavior. My David, it was embarrassing."

"Papa Charlie, I know. But even though I didn't see that dark side, I do remember there was something—I don't know quite what it was—that moved me. Perhaps it was the depression. She was a sad grandmother, and I was a sad boy. The last time I saw her—it was a Thursday night—I had a premonition that she was going to die."

Papa Charlie was shocked. "What do you mean?"

"She came to our house for dinner. She was in a horrible state: visibly agitated, smoking and eating at the same time, which she never did. It seemed as if she were screaming in some kind of silent code, 'Please, listen to me!' But nobody picked up on her desperation. The next day, on the way home from my piano lesson, I told my mom about my fear of Nana dying within the week. And she did—three days later."

"I'm sorry, my David, that you've had to keep that a secret all these years. I wish medication had been available during her lifetime. What a woman she could have been. What a woman she was meant to be."

"I know the community's memory of her is negative," I said. "But neither we nor they knew she was manic-depressive. She was misunderstood. But I don't care. I loved her. Sometimes I think I may feel her kind of sadness."

"And you should love her," Papa Charlie said. "She was your grandmother. Your troubled, gifted, honorable grandmother." Suddenly his face became stern. "I may sound old-fashioned, my David, but today, especially because of the divorce rates and other problems, my code of honor is that one always stays loyal to the family, no matter what. With special cases such as your grandmother, whom I really didn't understand medically until many years later, you have to remember that much of her erratic behavior was from a horrible, lifelong depression. In those days there weren't many treatments for it."

It seemed amazing to me that Leah had been able to get married, raise children, and function all those

decades, despite sixty-eight years of mostly unstoppa-
ble misery.

"I'm glad you were there for her," I said at last.

"I just wish she would have lived a little longer to
get the benefits of more modern medicine." Papa Charlie's face brightened for a moment. "She's probably smiling down on us because she recognized how we all felt
a long time ago." Suddenly he became reflective and
quizzical. "Perhaps it was a message."

"What do you mean?"

"That maybe Leah was a message from God."

I didn't understand. Didn't love and marriage mean
placing one's happiness in the happiness of another? Had
Papa Charlie, pained in his love, redirected some of his
emotions away from her?

"You see, my David, it's a complicated thing. Leah
forced me to make decisions I may not have made if
things had been different."

He seemed to retreat into himself, drifting into an
inner world that to me was still opaque. There were many
unanswered questions about both of them. Perhaps now
was the time to clarify the mystery that veiled his life
with Leah.

"If I had had a wife with a different temperament

. . ." The emotions came hard. "You see," he said softly, "I was unhappy much of the time. We both were."

These were painful words from my grandfather, whose optimism seemed otherwise unlimited.

"Oh, my David," he soothed, "don't look so sad. We had our difficulties. Still, Leah was also a great blessing to me—to all of us. There's an old Russian saying: 'To love deeply in one direction makes us more loving in all others.' This was Leah's gift to me."

Papa Charlie probably never heard of the Russian-born French author Madame Swetchine, who wrote that. Still, he proved the correctness of her wisdom in his community deeds. If Leah tested the infinite nature of love, she also inspired his charity. And I learned at last that in his struggles with my grandmother, the muse of his giving was born.

Seven

If Someone Isn't Quirky, It's Not a Family Vacation

 You couldn't say we were exactly model grandchildren, but at twelve my cousin Leslie and I thought we were pretty perfect.

Papa Charlie had invited us to spend a week with him in Miami Beach. It's true we didn't ruin his life or make him *completely* miserable in just seven days, but he should have known: Two against one equals no fun—for him.

The big fights were over food. Papa Charlie was completely absorbed by Adele Davis's books about nutrition. Leslie and I were entranced by mysteries and fiction. Already I could see that this was not going to be a *Jeopardy* match.

One afternoon the three of us were in Epicure, one of the great gourmet markets in Miami. What could I have been thinking when I asked Papa Charlie if he would buy me a frozen, *processed,* sugar-laden *thing?*

"Do you eat that kind of stuff at home?" he asked, more aghast than angry. To me it looked as if he were ready to sit shivah over it.

"Well, yes . . . sometimes."

He let it pass.

Then I saw a perfectly created Boston cream pie. It looked like a sculpture to me and my stomach.

"Papa Charlie, may I get a piece of . . . ?"

His eyes followed my finger. "David, wouldn't you rather eat a piece of fruit? Look at these huge oranges and grapefruits."

Beautiful. "I'd rather have the pie."

"But it's unhealthy."

"I don't care."

"Neither do I," Leslie agreed.

"It will raise your cholesterol," Papa Charlie retorted.

"So?" we replied in unison.

"Okay. How about if we go out for ice cream later? Is that a fair compromise?"

It was a lousy bargain, but we agreed to it. Later that night I opened Papa Charlie's refrigerator. I had to close it immediately. I was repulsed. Everything inside either had bones or you could see through it. I don't mind fish, but it does bother me when it stares back.

The next day Leslie and I made breakfast while Papa Charlie took his morning walk. Because he didn't eat eggs it was an easy assignment. We set his place at the table with a plate of black bread, a side of molasses, two glasses of warm milk, and two of hot water. Leslie and I had bagels with lox.

After the meal Papa Charlie asked us to clear away everything and wash the dishes.

"You mean scrape off the food and put the plates and stuff in the dishwasher?" I asked dumbly.

Leslie and I worked diligently to arrange everything neatly inside the dishwasher. Vaguely—very vaguely— I recalled that soap was already included in its cleaning cycle, but I was afraid to make that assumption.

I called Papa Charlie from the next room. "How do you use this thing?"

"Oh, that." He reached into the cabinet under the sink and handed me a yellow plastic bottle of liquid Joy. "Put some of this inside."

"Are you sure?"

"Of course I'm sure."

"Papa Charlie," I started timidly, "I think the soap is already included in the cycle."

"C'mon," he said. "Put some in."

I squirted the Joy inside and set the machine to "normal wash." Then we left for the rest of the day.

When we returned the kitchen was awash in bubbles. Leslie and I yanked off our socks and sneakers. "Where do we start?" I asked. Soap had leaked through the spaces around the machine like unclottable blood. Bubbles were flying to the ceiling and clinging to the walls.

"Clean this up, *please*," Papa Charlie said brusquely.

"Why are you mad at us? You said . . ."

"Never mind what I said. Please start cleaning."

I poured soap down one drain, and it came up the other. Suds were oozing through the sides of the dishwasher. I began to wonder if this soap monster was going to overtake us. Leslie opened the machine and dug through the frothy white mess like a miner. I stayed busy, keeping thoughts that were completely against my Myers-Briggs profile: I was having a positive attitude. And the dishes, it turned out, were the cleanest you ever saw.

We bailed water for hours. Finally the kitchen was

spotless, though Papa Charlie remained uncharacteristically grumpy for a while. Eventually he came back and apologized for blaming the whole disaster on us.

"Look, I have to take a piece of the blame," he confessed. "I wasn't clear with my instructions." Then he smiled as his eyes swept the kitchen. "You could say I blew it. But the lesson here is really simple: Blame is divisible by the number of people who don't understand something—but swear they do."

Eight

They Will Follow

*P*apa Charlie's childhood family was not close. He never formed adequate relationships with his siblings and did not wish to repeat the pattern with us. As a young man he promised himself that he would never perpetuate the mistakes his parents had made. When he married he vowed to create a family that was intimate and loving.

"There is nothing more important than children in a marriage. They give you life, something to carry on for," he said.

When my father was young, he and Papa Charlie used to bicycle on the Coney Island boardwalk, stop at a candy store, and sometimes visit Great-Grandmother Sadie. This was one of their weekly rituals.

When my aunt Arlene was a girl, Papa Charlie used to ask her opinions about all kinds of issues; he wanted to know what the world was like from a child's point of view.

"This made me feel very important," Arlene told me.

Through the years his relationship with each family member was special and separate. When the children and grandchildren married, their spouses were never just in-laws, and my mother and uncle became Papa Charlie's children as well.

"I have been blessed by my children and their marriages. This has given me great joy and inspiration," Papa Charlie used to say. "I have learned that if you build a good life and relationship with your children, they, in most cases, will follow your example. I have four children," he would say with pride to anyone who asked.

Their happiness, accomplishments, continuous love, and support inspired him to continue with philanthropic and educational causes that were important to him.

"You know, there is an old Jewish proverb that says, 'Parents used to teach their children to talk. Today children teach their parents to keep quiet.' It applies to me in this sense: Sometimes my children have more wisdom than I do, so I take their advice.

"I remember when we were starting the construction of the Jewish Community Center. I said to your parents that I wanted to pledge a certain amount of dollars. Bob Smith said to me, 'I think we should give more.' He named the figure. 'Now, that would be setting an *example!*' he said, and he was right. So I pledged the amount he recommended.

"My David, your parents, your aunt and uncle, and I are very close because we spend a lot of time together talking and discussing things. My mother and father didn't do that." He winced. "As a result, we never became close. We never took the time to find out what we had in common. Years later I used to say to myself, 'Charlie Smith, you're a fool for letting that happen.' But it did. What could I do? I was only a child. I am close to my children and grandchildren because I did not repeat those mistakes. It's important for you to have the same kind of closeness with your siblings, and later on with your wife and children. Anyone can do it. All you have to do is try. This is what love is all about."

Nine

Eyes

When Papa Charlie arrived in Washington, D.C., in 1942 with an opportunity to build homes in District Heights, he didn't know a single person in the city. He rented a room near Capitol Hill. In those days boarding-houses were plentiful. It was not uncommon for members of Congress or their staffers to live in rented rooms. But the city was hot—hotter than it is today. Buildings and homes were not air-conditioned. During the spring, fall, and winter the weather was agreeable and the Hill was stimulated by politics, politicians, and their families. But during the summer, when Washington's sweltering heat and humidity were at their zenith, most political families went home, leaving an uncomfortable quiet and a horrible haze of lethargy.

Papa Charlie was already lonely because his family

was still in Brooklyn, and he could visit them only about twice a month. At that time he was working for himself; it would be another four years before he created the Charles E. Smith Company.

Papa Charlie began looking for contractors for the District Heights project, which would consist of fifty-six lower-income homes. Each would sell for $4,500 with a $500 down payment.

"Since I wasn't familiar with the area, I looked in the yellow pages," he remembered.

But while he interviewed prospective jobbers and listened to what each had to say, Papa Charlie paid far more attention to the man's eyes.

"A person's eyes reveal his character. Eye contact is very important. If a man was looking to work for me, and he wouldn't look at me—he was finished! I wouldn't hire him."

He believed that eyes were what the great writers have called "the windows of the soul." They unveiled truth and motivation, regardless of a person's body language.

"The eyes are the mirrors that show a man's insides to the outside world," he said. "If he's paying close attention, the man looking in can never be tricked."

Over time his construction team was assembled, and although the project failed, the relationships did not. Many of the men who worked on those houses were hired by Papa Charlie when he formed his own company in 1946. Some of the acquaintanceships evolved into honed friendships. And none of the people he hired ever had to be fired. The eyes did indeed have it.

Ten

A Past Recast

$\mathcal{A}$ few months after the District Heights job was finished, Papa Charlie returned to Washington to close out the project. Now he needed a job. On his last day he grabbed a newspaper at the train station just before boarding for Brooklyn. He happened to glance through the want ads. By luck there was an opening for a construction superintendent at the T. X. Wax Companies, one of the largest builders in town. Papa Charlie immediately wrote a letter applying for the position, but within a couple of days he forgot about it.

Two weeks later a telegram arrived asking for an interview.

He took the early-morning train from New York in

order to be in Washington before noon. When he reached Mr. Wax's office in the LaSalle Building on Connecticut Avenue there were more than a dozen people waiting to be interviewed for the same job.

"I realized I would not be seen for some time and that Wax might hire someone before he even spoke to me," Papa Charlie told us. "I went up to his secretary and told her I had traveled from Brooklyn at Mr. Wax's request and that if he could see me within one hour I would wait. Otherwise I would go back home."

Fifteen minutes later Wax summoned Papa Charlie into his office.

"Tell me, Mr. Smith, why does a Jewish man such as yourself have an Anglo-Saxon name?" Wax asked bluntly.

Papa Charlie explained how "Schmidoff" had been changed to "Smith" when Reuven arrived in America. Wax made an incredulous face. They spent an hour together. Wax asked for references and told Papa Charlie he would hear from him soon. Two weeks later Papa Charlie received a telegram requesting another interview.

During that later meeting Papa Charlie discovered that his past had been investigated more thoroughly than he would have thought possible. Wax knew he had journeyed to America on the *Litania* as well as some of the details of his previous business experiences. Then he asked, "Why do you want this job?"

"It's very simple. I just finished a job here that wasn't very successful. My entire adult life has been spent in the construction business. I know how to build, and I know how to supervise."

"How much salary are you asking for?"

"I want one hundred and fifty dollars a week," Papa Charlie said.

"Let me remind you, Mr. Smith, that when you came here two weeks ago there were twelve or fifteen men downstairs who would gladly have taken this job for seventy-five dollars a week. Why should I pay you twice as much?"

Papa Charlie's eyes flashed. "Because if you hire one of them, they would probably do a good job, and for seventy-five dollars you'll get seventy-five dollars' worth of work. But if you hire me for one hundred fifty dollars, you'll get *three hundred dollars'* worth of work."

Wax hired Papa Charlie.

Eleven

The Second Cycle of Success

One afternoon in 1944 Papa Charlie was buzzed by his secretary, Miss Cherry: "Mr. Smith, a Mr. Sol Hurwitz is here to see you."

"I don't know him from a hole in the wall, but ask him in," Papa Charlie said.

Hurwitz sat down and lit a cigarette. He owned a profitable liquor store and lived in a nice house in northwest Washington, near the zoo.

"Mr. Smith, everyone in Washington is talking about you," he began.

"I find that hard to believe. I've lived here almost two years, and I still don't really know anyone. I live in southeast, and all of the Jewish families live in northwest. How can everyone be talking about me?"

"Because you're working for T. X. Wax, who doesn't sell or rent to Jews. You're also running a big project all by yourself. Tell me, why aren't you working for yourself?"

Papa Charlie smiled wanly. "It's very simple. I have no money."

"If that's your only problem," Hurwitz said, "we should have dinner soon and continue the conversation."

A few days later Papa Charlie and my grandmother arrived at the Hurwitzes' home for dinner. After the meal Hurwitz said, "Charlie, I want to go into business with you."

Papa Charlie sighed. "The building business requires an awful lot of money, Sol."

"That's no problem. I own a very successful liquor store and have all the money we would need."

"Let me tell you how we operate in New York," Papa Charlie explained. "If you furnish the money, you own a 50 percent interest. If I do the building, I get the other 50 percent."

They drew up the contract, which Hurwitz signed. Papa Charlie withheld his signature until he spoke to Wax.

Wax offered Papa Charlie a $25-a-week salary increase to stay on, which was a pinchpenny enticement even by 1944 standards. My grandfather remained silent. He wondered if there was a message here. He decided that a future with the T. X. Wax Companies was virtually no future at all.

"Mr. Wax, as you know, I was a successful builder in New York," Papa Charlie said at last. "If you allow me to become your partner, I could make a great deal of money for both of us."

Wax leaned back arrogantly in his leather chair and folded his hands. "Let me tell you something, Charlie. There are two things I will never share with anyone. One is my wife. The other is my business."

Papa Charlie's current workload for Wax was nearly completed. He gave his two weeks' notice, parted amicably, and signed the contract with Hurwitz.

Their first venture was a four-story apartment house in northwest Washington. When the building was completed, Papa Charlie found a ten-acre site nearby. He informed Hurwitz that he needed more money to carry on.

"Charlie," he replied, "I don't have any more money."

Papa Charlie was shocked. "But Sol, you told me you had all the money we needed!"

"Not to worry. I have a brother who has more money than I do."

George Hurwitz, Sol's younger sibling, owned a market in Virginia. He agreed to invest $25,000 in their next project. Each of the three would have an equal share in the ownership. When Papa Charlie was about to purchase the land, Sol told him that George too had run out of capital. But not to worry, he assured Papa Charlie. The Hurwitzes had a third brother, Morris, who was wealthier than all of them.

The deal was never consummated. Papa Charlie and the Hurwitzes dissolved their business relationship but remained friends for the rest of their lives.

"Papa Charlie, it sounds as if these guys didn't treat you very well," I said. "How could you be friends after that?"

"My David, the Hurwitzes didn't mistreat me at all. You must remember, though, that business is luck—but friendship is even luckier."

Twelve

I Told Them the Bad News, and They Invested Anyway

$\mathcal{P}$rior to 1960 the Charles E. Smith Company had built only apartment buildings. But in that year Papa Charlie decided to diversify by constructing an office building.

He met a gentleman who owned a desirable piece of land in downtown Washington who was willing to sell, and the deal was secured with a handshake.

Because this type of project requires more money to start, Papa Charlie decided to invite twelve people to a luncheon to discuss it. Yet as the day neared, he began to feel doubtful about the whole venture. Something told him that this brand-new project might be too risky. His potential investors could lose a lot if the property were not leased quickly, or they could make a lot of money with luck and timing. Papa Charlie wondered what to do.

"Bob, I think I should call off the meeting," Papa Charlie told my father. "I'm having second thoughts. Maybe this project is too big for us. What do you think?"

"Don't cancel it," my father advised. "Instead, why don't you just present the facts?"

"Okay, I'll do that."

So he walked to the podium and told the prospective investors the following with a poised posture and assured voice: The location of the building-to-be was poor because it was across the street from a funeral home and dilapidated housing. The construction would take at least a year, and because of the unstable economy there could be difficulty in leasing the space. In addition, each percentage of ownership would cost $100,000.

Surprisingly, the response was so overwhelming that within five minutes the partnership was sold out, and Papa Charlie exceeded his financial goal by $400,000.

His friends had done so well investing in his earlier ventures that they ignored the possible risks. They knew my grandfather had too much integrity to consider or offer a dubious deal.

The message from his inner voice had been worth

listening to, especially because his confidence in the project had been only intermittent. But with my father's support and all of the investors' he was ready to proceed.

Later he said, "Nerve succeeds—so long as it rides
on the truth."

Thirteen

The Sense of a Woman

*A*fter Papa Charlie's first Washington building project failed in 1942, his partner, Joe Snyder, offered him a chance to move to Bridgeport, Connecticut.

"Charlie, there's a bar and grill that I have an option to buy for one hundred thousand dollars. I will give you 50 percent interest in it with no investment if you agree to move to Connecticut to run it. Your salary would be three hundred a week. Leah would work five days a week, two hours a day, as the cashier. She would be paid fifty dollars a week. After a few years I'll sell for at least twice the money and give you half the profits."

"Joe, I appreciate your offer, and I like the deal. But let me discuss it further with Leah."

Leah was emphatic: "I am not interested, Charlie!"

"Dear, listen," he told her. "This is a wonderful opportunity. I'll make a lot of money. After a few years I can go back to the building business."

"No, Charlie. I don't want to leave Brooklyn. You are a builder, and that is the field in which you belong. Besides, I do not want to go from being the wife of a builder to being a cashier in a bar and grill. You'll find something better."

"How can you be so sure?"

"Because I have faith in you."

My grandmother's refusal to move led to another job opportunity in Washington and, later on, the formation of the Charles E. Smith Company.

By 1948 the Smith Company had built several successful apartment buildings whose management functions had been hired out. My father suggested that the company form its own team; it would be profitable, and the properties would be maintained at a higher standard.

Papa Charlie was not enthusiastic. Again he decided to consult Leah. She agreed with my father.

"Charlie, the building business is cyclical. A management company will give us more financial stability," she counseled.

"I liked and trusted what Leah had to say," Papa Charlie recalled. "I realized I could have consulted her on so many other decisions I had had to make on my own. She convinced me, and the management company was begun."

He looked at me, and his face became sad.

"Papa Charlie, what are you thinking?"

"That maybe I've missed something—something that was right there all the time."

"What do you mean?"

"Ask for advice from the person who knows you the best. Is it your spouse?"

Fourteen

I Quit

$\mathcal{I}$n 1967 Papa Charlie announced to my father and Uncle Bobby during lunch, "Fellows, as of tomorrow, I quit. I retire. I'm turning over the business to you."

They were astonished and a little taken aback. That day they appointed Papa Charlie chairman of the board. But in the twenty-eight years he was to live and hold the position, the board never convened.

His decision to quit was partially based on a recurring dream of seeing men high up on a scaffold, laying bricks. It was another of his "messages."

"At first I did not attach any importance to my dream, since it could have been a reflection of my daily activities as a builder," he explained. "But a few nights later I dreamed it again. I began to think that perhaps it had a message for me. When I tried to relate it to the Bible I remembered that while Jacob was working for his father-in-law he dreamed about black spots and white spots. He concluded that it was a sign from God that he was meant for more important things than tending sheep.

"The older man was astonished when Jacob announced his intention of leaving. But Jacob held fast to his plan. He had faith in his dream.

"I believed my dream meant that it was time for me to move on. I was not destined to remain a builder all my life. I realized that I had other important things to do."

At the lunch he reminded my father and Uncle Bobby that the community had been very good to him.

"I have made all the money I will ever need," he told them. "From now on I want to devote myself to more meaningful things."

The next morning Papa Charlie began his second career as a full-time philanthropist. He began by perusing the *Washington Post* for human-interest stories about persons in need. Over the years he used his Magic Marker many times to draw a circle around an article about a person or human situation that moved him.

Once he sent a washing machine to a poor woman who had numerous children. He helped friends who had trouble making rent payments. He lent money to employees. At then–Attorney General Robert Kennedy's request, Papa Charlie solicited the money to construct a swimming pool for Washington's Dunbar High School, which was in a poorer section of town.

This morning ritual of searching the newspaper was an important one that he maintained for decades, long after he had already raised millions of dollars for various causes.

A lot of my grandfather's friends said he taught them how to give. Papa Charlie believed in bestowing many of his gifts as quietly as possible on causes that were particularly humanitarian.

When people asked why he spent such a large portion of his life raising and donating money, his answer was deceptively simple: "The more money I give away, the better I feel."

Fifteen

Giving

*P*apa Charlie learned the great tradition of *tzedekah,* or giving charity, from his mother. From the time he was a child in Russia, Great-Grandmother Sadie kept a *pushke,* or metal-slotted box, which she filled with the money she saved from her household allowance. She would then turn it over to the synagogue to distribute to those in need.

Sixty years later Papa Charlie exposed his grandchildren to the world of philanthropy by taking us to black-tie dinners, telling us about his latest charitable projects, or including us in casual dinner conversation about them. We got to meet Golda Meir in 1968, when she presented him with the Prime Minister's Medal for Community Service, and again in 1970 while we were vacationing in Israel.

By the time we were teenagers Papa Charlie felt we were ready to act on the knowledge he had given us. He decided to dispense with conventional birthday presents and substitute checks, with a request that we give one-third of the gift to a cause of our choice.

One time I balked, selfishly. "Why don't you just give us 30 percent less money?" I wondered.

"Because you won't learn the lesson I am trying to teach," he answered patiently. "If you can't actually work for a cause, then by writing a check you at least *feel* what it's like to give away money. This is very important. I want you to experience the writing of your own check, the sealing of the envelope, the affixing of the stamp, and the posting of the letter."

The art, we learned, was in the giving.

Sixteen

Member of the Board Strikes a Chord

*I*n 1968 Papa Charlie was invited to become a member of George Washington University's board of directors. He turned down the offer.

"I'm just an ordinary citizen in Washington, DC. I'm not worthy of such an honor," he said.

Still, university officials were resolute about enticing him into service. They were trying to revitalize the board, and Papa Charlie would be perfect for the job.

Papa Charlie agreed to think it over. While pondering the offer, he was taken to lunch by friends who also happened to be associated with the school. They urged him to join.

After discussing it with the family, Papa Charlie agreed.

"Becoming part of an academic institution was a special privilege," he told me. But for the first time in his adult life he felt unequal to the stature of the group.

During the first few meetings he was reticent and self-conscious. Finally the board gave him an assignment he was sure he could accomplish: to serve as a member of the Development Committee, which had the task of raising money for a new medical school. Papa Charlie was particularly well qualified because earlier in the decade he had almost singlehandedly solicited the $10 million needed to fulfill his dream of building a Jewish Community Center, Jewish Social Service Agency, and Hebrew Home for the Aged—within one complex. This dream was attained despite initial skepticism from the community.

Lloyd Elliott, president of George Washington University, informed Papa Charlie that he was going to appoint Supreme Court Justice Tom Clark as chairman of the committee.

"Why are you making him chairman?"

"Because, Charlie, he's a big name. We want you to serve as vice chairman," Elliott explained.

"Sorry, I don't take vice-chairman jobs," Papa Charlie said tartly. "I'll end up doing all the work, so I'll just serve on the Development Committee."

At the next meeting representatives of a Pittsburgh-based fund-raising company were present.

"I listened as they read from a list of foundations we were expected to solicit," Papa Charlie recalled. "I didn't choose any of them. I didn't know anyone at those foundations."

Two weeks later a report of "no progress" was given. Not one committee member had been successful in his solicitations. The Pittsburgh people distributed a second list of foundations, instructing the committee to contact the new groups. Again Papa Charlie did not take down any names.

The committee members reported that they had been unsuccessful at the following meeting as well. Nearly a year passed without any triumphs. Finally Papa Charlie, who had remained almost silent during the series of meetings, spoke up.

"I don't see why you're distributing the names of more foundations since you have raised no money from the previous lists, and apparently they were the best," he said to the fund-raisers and the board.

"But we have to keep trying," one of the professionals replied.

"I think you're wasting time and money," Papa Charlie retorted.

"What do you suggest we do?"

"First thing—fire the fund-raisers! They're costing us a lot of money, and we aren't getting anywhere."

The comment halted the meeting. Everybody left the room except Papa Charlie and Elliott.

"Okay, Charlie, what now?" Elliott was impatient and frustrated. "George Washington has been trying to build the new medical school for years. There have been many setbacks, and now I've lost my fund-raisers!"

"I'll tell you what we're going to do," Papa Charlie replied. "I know a good fund-raiser in Washington. He can handle the whole thing, and I'll help him."

"Who is he?" Elliott asked.

"Dr. Seymour Alpert."

Elliott was incredulous. "I'm afraid Dr. Alpert has strained relationships with some of the doctors in the community because of past solicitations."

"Sometimes you have to antagonize people," Papa Charlie explained. "You *make* them give what they *should* give, not what they *think* they should give."

Several weeks later Elliott asked Alpert to take over

the chairman's job. Alpert then met privately with Papa Charlie. They were close friends who had worked together on other community projects.

"Charlie, I'm not an experienced fund-raiser," Alpert confessed. "I don't know if I can accept this offer to chair the Development Committee."

"Sy, they're asking you to do something different from anything you've ever done. You're a professor of anesthesiology. That's a great field. Now you've been asked to be chair of a committee to raise money. You'll travel and meet new people. I think you're the right professional for the job. Please think about it very carefully before you make your final decision."

Alpert accepted the job, and Papa Charlie was delighted.

"Sy, I think the first thing you should do is find twenty members of the board who will pledge a minimum of twenty-five thousand dollars each. We'll invite them to a luncheon and explain our financial needs."

A few weeks later, during a gathering at the Madison Hotel, the directors were told about the $10 million that had to be pledged within three months to qualify for a $14 million match from the government. The total cost was estimated to be $26 million.

During his speech Papa Charlie quoted Dr. Abbott

Lowell, a former Harvard president who had said that universities must be beggars, and the harder they beg the more successful they will be. Papa Charlie looked at his audience intensely: "As of today, we are beggars too."

By the end of the afternoon more than $1 million had been committed. Later that month the doctors from the medical school pledged another $1 million. The $10 million required to qualify for the matching funds was secured within the deadline.

The new medical school was completed in 1973—without a mortgage.

"You know what, my David?" Papa Charlie told me. "If you ever want to get anything accomplished, don't wait for a consensus. *Tsedokeh zol kein geltnit kosten un g'milas-chassodim kain agmas-nefesh nit farshafen, volten geven in der velt fil tsadikim.*"

"What does that mean?" I asked.

"It's an old Yiddish saying: If one could do charity without money and favors without aggravation, the world would be full of saints."

Seventeen

He Opened My Mind, and I Learned about My Brain

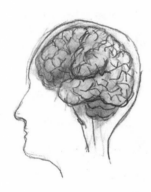 early thirty years ago, during a flight to Israel, Papa Charlie learned about psychobiology.

"What the heck is that? I never heard of the word," he said to his friend Dr. Joel Elkes.

"Body and mind working together," Joel replied.

Papa Charlie wanted to know all about it.

"The mind and body are not separate entities. They function as one coordinated unit," Dr. Elkes explained.

As he learned more, Papa Charlie became so enthusiastic that he wanted to start a psychobiology institute in Israel that would study the science of the brain. His interest in this subject may have been partly related to my grandmother's psychological difficulties; by 1971 some of her episodes were so serious that she needed sedation to tolerate them.

When he returned home, he consulted the family. My parents, Uncle Bobby, and Aunt Arlene were enthusiastic about the idea. The following year the Institute of Psychobiology was cofounded by Papa Charlie and Joel.

Papa Charlie told us, "I am going to ask them to create a Memory Pill for me. My memory is terrible—terrible!"

Each year when he returned to Jerusalem for the institute's board meetings, he would ask about progress on his pill. He waited twenty-four years.

"Fortunately, I'm not too disappointed," he said when the pill did not materialize. "If my Memory Pill is not discovered in my lifetime, so be it. Maybe my grandchildren and great-grandchildren will benefit from it. At least I've gotten exposure to the world of science, an area that I would never have known about had it not been for Joel."

His pill may never be fashioned because of the enormous cost. But in the intervening years the institute's scientists have become internationally known for their discoveries in mental illness, including Gulf War syndrome, and psychopharmacology—achievements Papa Charlie lived to see.

Before and since Papa Charlie's death, I have had

the honor of holding the title of president of the institute. My responsibilities are to preside over the annual board meeting, attend the annual Charles E. Smith Lecture, and approve the budget. I've loved it.

And there was always Papa Charlie's encouragement: "Never be afraid to delve into a subject you know nothing about," he advised. "You will either discover an aptitude or, at the very worst, you won't like it."

Eighteen

Fa Klempt at Sea

You know that Dickens novel that begins, "It was the best of times, it was the worst of times . . . ?" Well, the French Revolution would probably have been less traumatic for me than my short and miserable history at sea with a fish, a green grandfather, and some other nice, normal people.

You see, the guillotine is the easy way to go when you're in the midst of the infamous *mal de mer* because you want to die anyway, so why not make it quick: chop-chop? Instead it just drags on and on.

Papa Charlie, my cousin Leslie, and I were in Florida. We had been invited to spend the day aboard a friend's boat in Key West.

How could I have known this experience would be so miserable? The only thing I knew about boats was from watching *Flipper*, and the one other time I had gone deep-sea fishing was aboard the sleek *Alexandra-Max* on the Chesapeake Bay. The waves were huge that day, but I caught nineteen fish without even a twinge of nausea. So why would I have anxiety about doing it again? Maybe that was my mistake. I should have put on my backup, what-if-something-happens-oh-my-*God*! system.

I was feeling great as we boarded the magnificently purple *Daisy IV*. It was nearly 80 degrees. The sky was azure, the water was still, and my thirteen-year-old stomach was filled to capacity with fried eggs, bacon, and bagels. Leslie and I had gone to breakfast by ourselves, so Papa Charlie didn't know that I had clogged my arteries and eaten *trayf*.

Our host, Captain Gunther, welcomed us. He was a longtime friend of the family who had survived the Holocaust by painting signs. After World War II he came to America and started a successful company that specialized in the same craft. Papa Charlie had a thirty-year business relationship and friendship with him.

All of us were excited about catching a lot of fish.

"Any whales in these waters?" I asked stupidly.

"Not here. We're in the Florida Keys, not way out in the ocean," Gunther said.

Good. I don't feel like wrestling with one of them, or a humongous shark either.

"What have you got?" I asked. Gunther looked puzzled. "I mean by way of fish."

"Oh. You mean in small, tame fishes, or in the mean shark-barracuda variety?"

"Mean would be nice." *What am I thinking? Do I really want to go up against some angry, voracious sea monster?*

He helped me cast my line into the water and put the rod into the holder.

"Barracuda—lots of 'em out here," he said dramatically.

I screeched back my chair. *"Barracuda?* You mean like barracuda on a bagel?"

"Well, the meat's a little tough. Don't worry, there's plenty of fish in the sea."

He started the engine, and from my lounge chair I watched with wonder as the sun reflected against the water and created a spectrum of hues. There was a slight breeze. I closed my eyes and thought, *This is going to be nice.*

After we had been cruising for about twenty

minutes, I noticed Papa Charlie fiddling with a small yellow cardboard box.

"What's that?" I asked.

"Oh, this? It's Dramamine," he replied casually.

"Drama-what?"

"For seasickness," he mumbled.

"I've never seen you seasick before."

"That's because I always take this stuff before I board. I've only been sick on a boat once before."

"When?"

"In 1911, while crossing the Atlantic to come to this country."

Papa Charlie's father, Reuven, had left for New York in 1908 to learn the building trade from his brother Max. The rest of the family had remained in Russia. Finally, after a three-year separation, Reuven had saved enough money to send for them.

"We left from Latvia aboard the *Litania*. The ship seemed so big," Papa Charlie recalled. "Of course it wasn't; it just looked that way to a kid. In those days they didn't have the luxury liners they have now. Believe me, it was a rough four-week crossing. But the thought of being together again kept us going."

Papa Charlie's family had been luckier than most because Reuven had bought them second-class passage;

he was proud that he could afford it and keep everyone out of steerage.

"We ran around the decks and stuffed ourselves because we had never seen so much food," Papa Charlie continued. "We'd never eaten like that in our lives. I got sick from it, the weather, and the smell of garlic."

"Garlic? What do you mean?" I wondered.

"In those days Jews wore garlands of garlic to ward off the evil spirits and seasickness."

"Did it work?" I asked.

"I don't know. I saw an awful lot of nauseated people hanging over the rails. It didn't work with me, that's for sure."

"What a story! Knowing that, how could you ever forget to take your Dramamine?" I asked.

"I just forgot."

"Let me see that box." He handed it to me, and, curious, I read the directions. "It says here that . . ." I looked up. Papa Charlie's face was yellow-green.

"What does it say?" he asked weakly.

"Well, it says you have to take the first dose *before* you get on the boat."

He rose slowly out of his chair and stumbled toward the belowdecks.

"Charlie!" Gunther called. Papa Charlie turned,

wordless. His face was now ashen. "Don't go below. It only makes it worse," Gunther warned.

But Papa Charlie waved him away, and I watched anxiously as he clumpety-clumped his way belowdecks.

I turned to Gunther. "What do we do now?"

"Nothing. Just wait for Charlie—and the fish."

Suddenly Leslie appeared beside me. "David, are you hungry?" she asked in a cheerful, unconcerned voice.

I shook my head. Food was the last thing I wanted.

"Will you hand me a sandwich, please?"

"How can you eat now with Papa Charlie about to vomit?"

"I'm starving!" she exclaimed.

"The thought of food . . ." I muttered. I couldn't even look at it. I handed her the portable cooler. "All yours."

At first the ride proceeded smoothly. The greens and golds of the sun curved over the horizon. It was a strange sensation. The boat, which only an hour ago had seemed so big and sturdy, was now only a speck in the huge blue matrix of the sea. The wind piped up, and the boat started to rock with the long, white-capped waves.

Gunther stared at me. The boat climbed into a wave and jolted.

"I thought these waters were like glass," I said meekly.

"It's just a hiccup," Gunther laughed. "You can handle it."

"Hiccup? It's more like a roller coaster to me!"

"Don't worry," he soothed. "You'll grow some sea legs. Besides, I wouldn't be out here if it was too rough."

The waves grew larger and more rapid. Spray sliced across the bow. I looked out at the rising sea. *I'm not getting sick,* I told myself. *Maybe a fish will jump or something. Anything to distract me.* Nothing . . . nothing but blue. A larger wave rolled beneath the hull at a precipitous angle. My stomach lurched. I tried to focus: *You will not get sick; you will not get sick; you will not give in.* I gritted my teeth and tried to compose myself.

"Gunther, what's happening here?"

"Nothing; this is nothing," he tried to calm me.

I know why these waves are coming. These waves are coming because I ate trayf *for breakfast. I'm being punished!*

"I think I'm getting sick," I groaned.

"You're not going to puke, are you?" Leslie asked, annoyed.

"God, I hope not."

"Listen," Gunther counseled. "Lie back and take some deep breaths very slowly and calm yourself. You're getting worked up for nothing."

That's what you think.

Gunther got up from his chair. "Relax," he said soothingly. "Watch me. Take slow, deep breaths."

I inhaled, exhaled, inhaled again. "I feel queasy," I told him.

"Look at the horizon. Just fix on that imaginary line—nothing else. Now, concentrate on that line only. Do that and you'll steady yourself."

After a few minutes I said, "I think I'll go below and lie down."

"David, *please*, look at the horizon."

"No; I have to go below."

"That'll only make it worse," Gunther cautioned. "You really feel it down there, and the air isn't fresh."

"Impossible." He knew what he was talking about, but I was too green to listen.

When I finally made it to the bunk and closed my eyes, all I saw was a profusion of psychedelic images of seasick people. I blinked; they were spinning. I blinked again; there were more of them, reeling. I felt the ocean grow rougher, and then I passed out.

I have no idea how much time passed before I heard a voice.

"David, you have a bite on your line."

At first I didn't recognize it. I opened my eyes. There

was the voice again, and I answered feebly, "Reel it in for me, will you? If it's a caviar or a lox, keep it. If not, throw it back."

I didn't realize that just before I fell asleep Papa Charlie had left and returned to the upper deck. I closed my eyes again and tried to remain motionless. The cabin was pirouetting. When I opened my eyes Leslie was beside my bunk, smiling.

I lifted my body unsteadily. "What?" I lamented.

"You got a bite," she said.

"Then I wasn't imagining it?"

"What do you mean?" Leslie asked.

"I heard a voice telling me I had a bite, but I half thought I was hearing things."

She smiled. "Oh, you weren't imagining it."

"Who was it?"

"It was Papa Charlie."

At that moment I heard footsteps coming toward me. It was Papa Charlie, smiling.

"Remember that tug on your line?" he asked.

"Vaguely."

"It was a barracuda."

"Who reeled it in?"

"I did," he said proudly.

"But I thought you were sick."

"I was, but then you came down here and fainted. I was startled. I immediately put you to bed and realized that I had to make sure you were okay. I was feeling better and went topside. A few minutes later I called you. But you didn't answer, so I caught the fish for you. It's in Gunther's cooler. Leslie caught one too."

"But Papa Charlie, how did you recover so quickly?"

"Adrenaline. And the rest I guess I slept off."

Gunther was waiting for us. He was a good sailor, patient and familiar with the anxieties of a landlubber.

"Actually the sea is pretty calm—not bad at all," he remarked. "You and Charlie panicked when you felt a little motion. Happens all the time to people who aren't used to it."

Talk about losing your dignity. I collected myself and tried to sound happy. "I want to see what these barracudas look like," I said with faux bravado.

Gunther escorted me to the upper deck. A pair of long, silvery fish were lying side by side on a mound of ice, hooked and very dead.

"Snarly looking," I stated. "And those teeth; I've never seen such teeth."

"They use them like thin razors to cut through whole schools of fish," Gunther explained.

"Well, it's a *meeskite* fish if I ever saw one," Papa Charlie said. "Looks like the policeman in our village back in Russia."

"Look at them again," Gunther suggested. "They're really quite beautiful."

I looked at my barracuda. "Beautiful? Fabergé is beautiful. This is not beautiful."

"Gunther, will you please take a picture of us and our buddies?" I asked, removing my fish from the ice. Leslie picked up her catch, which was equally long, scaly, cold, and dead.

He focused the lens and pressed the shutter.

Papa Charlie laughed.

"What's so funny?" I asked.

"Well, now I've seen everything. It takes a special kind of person to change from seasickness one minute to taking a picture with his fish the next. I guess you could say that if you're ever in a situation, my David, where you can't find the humor in casual agony, move on. You'll have bigger fish to fry."

Nineteen

Yiskor, Biskor; You Don't Outsmart the Lord, Mister!

 **W**hen Reuven left for America in 1908, Papa Charlie became, at the age of seven, the little man of the family. He rose an hour before the rest of the household to light the wood-burning stove. He prepared his mother's coffee, took the long walk to the well, filled the buckets with water, and returned them to the kitchen. He never fell out of this role.

After the family reunited in America three years later, Papa Charlie took a number of jobs such as movie usher, Cracker Jack factory worker who put the prize in each box, Western Union delivery boy, and machinist.

When Reuven was diagnosed with cancer of the esophagus in 1925, Papa Charlie spent the most time with him, feeding him rice gruel and witnessing the burning effects and pain of the X-ray treatments. Sometimes, when Reuven couldn't talk, they just sat in silence holding hands for hours.

But when Papa Charlie was told that his father had died, he was terribly traumatized.

"I fell to the ground. I was unconscious for fifteen minutes. They couldn't wake me. I was totally and completely unconscious. Finally, when I came to, I thought, 'Oh my God, here I am, head of the family and the only one who can support the family.' So I supported my sisters, my brother, and my mother for the rest of their lives."

During the next eleven months, as is customary in Judaism, Papa Charlie attended synagogue every day to observe *Yiskor*, the prayer for the deceased.

For decades he observed his father's *Yiskor*. He never missed the service on the anniversary of Reuven's death except once, years later. It happened while he was vacationing on a Caribbean island where there was no synagogue. On the *Yiskor* day Papa Charlie decided to go snorkeling with a group from his hotel. After a few minutes of swimming he spotted two rocks ahead that were at least fifty feet apart. For someone with little experience in deep ocean water it was a terrifying sight. Papa Charlie panicked.

"I thought I'd never be able to swim through those rocks," he told us. "I started swallowing water and sinking. Luckily, the captain of the boat heard my cries for help. He pulled me out of the water and saved my life. I wondered why I felt such sudden and inexplicable terror and decided this was a message: I vowed never again to try to outsmart God."

He never missed *Yiskor* again.

Twenty

Eat Right, Stay Fit, but *Please* Pass Me a Potato Chip

*M*y mother was in the kitchen talking on the telephone with Papa Charlie—not chit-chatting as most fathers-in-law and daughters-in-law do. They were *discussing* because they were close and had many mutual interests.

Today I could hear them from the family room, blabbing about it again: *nutrition*. Not an uncommon subject in this house. They tossed Adele Davis's name around as fluently as I had once traded my beloved *Batman* cards.

You see, my family was basically normal, but we looked very peculiar to outsiders. We were thin; we exercised; but I at least always looked a bit distracted.

During the 1970s we didn't eat like the rest of

America—and neither did the rest of America when it ate with us. We lived through swallowing healthy, sawdust-tasting stuff because of my mother and Papa Charlie. I can say now that they were pioneers, but at the time, living with them ... well, it was not always a bargain. A good, conscientious mother can be an inconvenience.

But Mom had a mission: to protect us and herself against the pervasive heart disease that was on her side of the family. My maternal grandfather, Papa Shea, and all of his siblings had died of heart attacks. So there she was, her books and articles always piled up and annotated so she could stamp out the coronary risk factor.

And she did, all right, by limiting us to three eggs a week—or fewer. If you weren't looking, the yolk was cut out. Mom brought only polyunsaturated oil into the house, meaning safflower; any other kinds (peanut, coconut, palm, Crisco) were positively forbidden.

So I had a nutritionally challenged childhood. I read more about fat grams and the annals of cholesterol than the Old Testament. And believe me, none of my friends were living like this. They didn't even know what a low-fat-roughage-ridden-riddled-with-wheat-germ diet was.

I was an enigma at school. People thought I was strange; there was a rumor that I kept a pinup of Adele

Davis in my locker. Some of the eggheads even thought Holden Caulfield was my alter ego. But honest, I was quite integrated. I wasn't having a mental collapse like Holden. I was *hungry*.

Other kids were allowed to let Red Dye No. 3, cyclamates, nitrates, nitrites, MSG, and other preservatives pass freely through them. Not me. I was schlepping back and forth to the grocery store, learning how to read the ingredients on the canned foods that were acceptable in the house. Once I was so desperate I considered serving mayonnaise as a vegetable.

And my school lunch box was just as ascetic: tuna fish on wheat or some obscure grain bread, a neatly pared piece of fruit, and when available a sliver of low-fat cheese.

Somehow this atmosphere contradicted what my Jewish grandmothers preached to me whenever I visited their houses: "Eat! Eat! Eat!"

And when Mom wasn't looking, I did.

I thought food was a psychological substitute for the average teenager, who often feels a lack of love, security, and warmth. Wasn't it part of the hormonal, coming-of-age mess? The armor, so to speak?

Not in my house. Food was . . . something *else*.

Fortunately for her, Mom's concerns were soundly reinforced by Papa Charlie, who was practicing the same principles for completely different reasons. At sixty he underwent an epiphany, deciding almost overnight that if he abdicated his then-normal diet for twigs and vegetables he would live better and longer.

Papa Charlie thus had a monumental passage in his sixth decade. He banned frozen and sugar-containing foods from his life and replaced them with plain fish, and by that I mean the barely dead, white, prepared-without-salt-and-pepper, watery-tasting species. And vegetables. Because they had to be fresh, they were always steamed. They tasted like crunchy screws. The first thing I did when I came home from dinner at his house was eat.

Papa Charlie's passion about nutrition was all about retarding his aging. And he succeeded.

Now, I agree that healthy food is a nice thing in theory, but the rest of the family—my father; my siblings, Michelle and Steven; and I—were not always as enthusiastic as Mom. Mother Hubbard's cupboards, you could say, were so bare of junk that we almost went into family counseling. Eventually, though, Mom did agree to buy one or two Oreos and a chip here and there. She was a good sport.

And oh, how I yearned for that occasional bag of chips. To hear the crinkling of a Cheez Doodles bag was next door to an aphrodisiac!

Mom and Papa Charlie were still on the telephone when I suddenly walked into the kitchen and cut into their conversation.

"Can I have some junk?" I asked.

She frowned ever so slightly and shook her blond head: *No!*

So what could I do? I sat down and listened to them yap about the virtues of unbleached versus bleached flour, whole wheat versus white bread. What Mom didn't realize was that this house hadn't seen anything white in the last five years except paint.

"Your grandfather wants to know if you're eating well," she said.

"I'm eating," I said weakly.

"He says that contrary to all the reports you read, roughage actually does help a bad stomach. Are you eating salad and wheat cereal?"

"No." *Who wants to eat that?*

She mumbled something into the telephone and turned to me. "Papa Charlie says you need to eat right to look and feel good."

Bully. "Papa Charlie is seventy-three and I'm sixteen," I cried. "Don't I have a little time between now and arteriosclerosis?"

"No, you do not!" she snapped. "I read the study to all of you at the dinner table the other night. Autopsies of eighteen-year-old soldiers showed plaques in their arteries already. You don't wake up at forty and decide you're going to eat healthy."

"Let me talk to him." I practically grabbed the telephone. "Papa Charlie, what are you telling Mom? We're already the oddest family in America. We don't eat charcoaled steak because she says the carbon causes cancer. She cuts away our egg yolks. She takes the sugar out of the recipes. Have you ever had crêpes suzette *without* the suzette? It's like trying to start a fire without a flame."

"Good! Smart woman! You'll live longer on that diet," said Papa Charlie. "And in about twenty years you'll be grateful to us for teaching you good eating habits. Not only that, you'll be healthier than all your friends. I was just telling your mother that some fishes have oils that are believed to be good for your heart. But it has to be fresh fish, not canned."

"Well, you know me. I love caviar," I said sarcastically.

"My David, don't be funny. This is important. Someday when all of this is common knowledge, you'll be way ahead of everyone else."

Big deal. "The rest of this house wants steak and potatoes and macaroni and cheese and Milky Ways. We're sick of boiled chicken, cucumber or carrot soup, and cooked bananas. I'm losing weight every week."

"Last time I saw you, you looked terrific."

"But do I have to be miserable in the meantime? I mean, between now and the time the rest of the world is eating like this?"

"You're exaggerating, my David."

"No, I'm not." *I'm the new poster boy for Weight Watchers, and I didn't even have to go on a diet.*

Mom grabbed the receiver and spoke briskly into it. "Dad, I'll call you back later." She hung up.

"Listen, Mom, I really appreciate what you're trying to do. We all do. But could you lay off a little bit?"

She looked at me quizzically. "I don't understand."

"Let me explain. You see, guys my age are supposed to be obsessed with girls and have misdirected anger toward their parents and the world, SAT anxiety, fear of academic failure, and a general heavy gloom about the future."

"And?"

"I'm not worrying about any of those things. Instead I crave junk—you know, Fritos. Chips. Big Macs. Ice cream. Twinkies."

"I get the picture," she said flatly.

"Do you know what I did on the night of my prom?"

"Well . . . I assume you went to the dance."

"Shirley and I never left the restaurant. Instead, I *pigged out!*"

"*Oy vay*. Did you add creamer to your coffee?"

I nodded.

"Cremora?"

"Yes."

She hung her head. "The worst of them all. You couldn't have used 2 percent?"

"That's not the point."

"You're right," she sighed. "I've been on a mission to save us all. I guess if you're Papa Charlie's age you have less time to make an impact. But we do have time. You're learning—all of us are. You might not always follow what I say, but someday you will, I'm sure. So I'll moderate my zeal. That's what I'll do."

I kissed her. "Mom, you're the *greatest!*"

As Papa Charlie said: The art of how to eat is a feat.

Twenty-one

The Dating Game, Fifty Years Later

When Papa Charlie started to date after my grandmother's death in 1972, he was sad but practical. He did not wish to grow old alone. His children assured him that he could live with either of them, and with independence, but he wanted to remain in his own home.

Nearly half a century had passed since my grandfather had been on a date, yet the rhythm of romance came when the time was appropriate for him. Papa Charlie was a confident, dapper, gentlemanly escort who had busier Friday and Saturday nights than some of his socially active grandchildren. With various lady friends he widened his repertoire of restaurants, theaters, and films.

Most of these women we never met, though I do remember the lipsticked Natasha, a buxom Russian with a lyrical accent who once came to a family dinner. She was succeeded by Zelda, his most significant other, whom he courted for three years. She was worldly, traveled, educated, and an excellent bridge player—an interest she gave him for the rest of his life. But Zelda was a three-time divorcée who hoped to be Papa Charlie's fourth wife. My grandfather had pledged to the family that he would not marry someone of whom we did not approve, and already he was hearing, "She has some qualities that . . . well, you know . . ." Or, "Papa Charlie, we don't think Zelda is . . . uh, how can I put it . . . ?"

And so with that, and his own doubts, the relationship eventually ended. But Papa Charlie, always philosophical about his losses, declared, "It is God's will. Perhaps He is sending me a message."

Six months later Papa Charlie met Micki, whom everyone loved. Immediately.

But none of us could ever have anticipated the big surprise that was to unfold in that relationship. We would learn that not all of Papa Charlie's "messages" were the same.

Twenty-two

The Dove Was a Sign of Love

*A*fter two and a half years of widowerhood, Papa Charlie decided he wanted to remarry.

"I have courted many nice women since your grandmother died," he told me, "but not the right wife. It's time to find her."

The family had met only a few of his girlfriends. The longest relationship had been three years with Zelda, but no one except me had really cared for her; my parents, siblings, and other family members thought she was selfish. Papa Charlie continued to see her a little longer because I asked him to. After a few months he terminated their romance because his misgivings about her started to escalate.

One cool March morning shortly after that resolution, Papa Charlie asked his gardener, Sam, to begin preparations for the spring. Several days later Sam called Papa Charlie at his office and exclaimed, "Mr. Smith, there is a dove nesting in your magnolia tree!"

Incredulous, Papa Charlie went home that afternoon and looked for the bird, at first without success. Then, scanning with his binoculars, Papa Charlie saw a beautiful white dove snuggling in a small tangle of branches.

"I thought to myself: Why a dove? I'd never seen a dove in Washington. Why would a dove nest in my tree? After all, I had only one tree in my yard; the neighbors had dozens of them. Then I said to myself: This must be a message from God."

Papa Charlie took his afternoon nap, hoping some explanation would come to him. But when he awoke he was still mystified. Then he remembered the biblical story of Noah and the Great Flood. Noah had sent a bird to check the water's height, but it never returned. Later he dispatched a dove, which came back with a twig, a sign that the waters were receding and land was near.

That evening Papa Charlie called my aunt and told her the news.

"Honey, within thirty days there will be a dove coming into my life, and that will be the girl I marry."

The following Friday night Papa Charlie told the rest of the family about the dove and his interpretation of it. Although some were skeptical, he—wiser than most—paid no attention.

Two weeks later Papa Charlie's good friend of nearly thirty years, Miriam, called and said, "Charlie, your birthday is coming up. I'm planning on having a party for you."

He was not enthusiastic. "Miriam, birthday parties are just for children."

"I am planning the party!" she insisted.

"How about if you, Irving, and I celebrate my seventy-fourth birthday with a fancy dinner and some champagne? We'll have a great time."

"No, Charlie. I am making the birthday party for you."

Papa Charlie relented. There were many guests that night, and at first he was sure he had made a mistake agreeing to attend, but he was about to be surprised. Not long afterward, he explained what happened that evening. "My David, when it was time to sit down to dinner, I took one look at the woman beside me and thought, 'That is my dove!' "

She was a beautiful woman named Micki whose husband had died shortly before my grandmother. Papa

Charlie knew of her vaguely because his friend Dr. Joel Elkes had courted her.

"The first thing I asked her was if she was going steady with anyone. She looked at me, a little stunned, and said softly, 'No, I am not.' "

"You actually said *that* to her? That takes chutzpah!" I said.

"So then I said to her, 'Suppose I call you some evening and invite you out to dinner. Would you go?'

" 'I would like that,' she said."

When Papa Charlie arrived home he called my aunt again.

"Honey," he said, "the dove has come into my life. I have met the girl I am going to marry."

"But Dad, how do you know she is going to want to marry you?"

"What do you mean, how do I know? She is ordained from God!"

Papa Charlie and Micki started dating almost immediately. She was lovely, kind, gentle, and gracious—the perfect person for him. Finally it seemed he had discovered someone who completely complemented his needs. That sensitivity was apparent in their passion for each other. I'd never seen him demonstrative with a woman his age.

He proposed three months later, and Micki accepted. Then he started to accumulate doubts.

"Here I am rather old in age, marrying a woman nineteen years younger than me," he told me. "So I said to Micki that I felt slightly guilty about the whole thing. Before many years she may have to take care of an old man. What benefit is that? I told her I'd check into the Mayo Clinic, where I have been a patient for many years, and have a complete physical. Then I'll arrange for my doctors to send her a report."

Micki was surprised. "It really isn't necessary to go through all that trouble," she said.

Papa Charlie flew to the clinic. At the end of three days of examinations, the doctor concluded his health was equivalent to that of a man twenty-five years younger. He was elated.

"Do you really mean that?" Papa Charlie asked the doctor.

"Absolutely," his internist replied.

That evening Papa Charlie called Micki, enraptured. "Honey, I just completed the examination and the doctor says my health is equal to that of a fifty-year-old man. Now, do you think you are too old for me?" he joked.

"Well, I'm trying very hard to keep up with you," she laughed.

Five months later they were married at my parents' home. After a sumptuous brunch planned by my mother, they left for their honeymoon in San Francisco and Hawaii.

Papa Charlie's message to his skeptics was characteristically simple and proud: "If you think you're in love, don't ignore those messages from within—or above."

Twenty-three

Fountain of Youth— The Hard Way

 After Papa Charlie married Micki he became more flexible in his travel destinations and in the ways he chose to stay young and sexy.

One of the journeys he and Micki took was to an elegant spa in Baden-Baden of Nazi concentration camp notoriety. I didn't like the sound of this at all. Perhaps he didn't know? I thought maybe the color separations in the brochure had overwhelmed him.

I couldn't believe that my pro–Jewish education, anti-assimilation, Israeli-minded-but-living-in-the-dias-pora grandfather could visit such a place. When I told him of my objections he waved me away, either because his hearing was bad or because he didn't want to listen.

So, I thought, disgustedly, *Go off and relax among those Jewish ghosts and enjoy yourselves!*

"So, how was the spa?" I asked when he returned.

"Very, very elegant," he beamed.

"And?"

"Micki and I enjoyed ourselves *very* much." His brown eyes sparkled; his body was youthful and vigorous. There was a certain coy, playful lilt in his voice.

"How was Baden-Baden?" I asked, frowning.

"They gave us injections."

Oy vay! They tried to kill them, yet. "Injections?"

"Injections of lamb embryo."

Meshuga people. Probably leftover needles from World War II. "What? Is this a joke?" I frowned.

"They're supposed to make you feel younger," he said.

"Well? Did it work?"

He shook his head. "Not exactly."

"Papa Charlie, what did these shots do to you?"

He looked at me for a long time before he laughed. "They gave me a sore ass."

"So what good was the trip?"

His eyes gleamed impishly. "Just because I'm eighty-five doesn't mean I'm too old to think young."

"Papa Charlie, maybe I just don't get it."

He laughed himself to the edge of tears.

When he finally settled down he said, "My David, you're a young man. All that love requires is easy for you. But let me tell you that at my age the only true gift of love is in giving a portion of yourself. When you're sure of being loved, and you're old, it's not a bad thing to be very bold."

Twenty-four

Divorcé

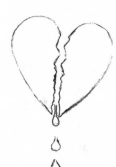

When he was eighty-six, Papa Charlie's beloved "Dove," Micki, asked for a trial separation.

The family was astounded. We had been so sure of her in the beginning. What had gone wrong?

I visited him at his office after I heard the news.

"Papa Charlie, what happened? Where is she?"

"The Westin Hotel."

His revived youthfulness of Baden-Baden now seemed to melt shapelessly into his chair.

"How long will she be there?" I asked.

"Three months." He shrugged. "But who knows . . ."

"Three months? Is that what she's asked for?"

He nodded.

"Why so long?"

"It isn't so long, really," he sighed.

His words surprised me. At age eighty-six, three months might as well have been forever.

"Papa Charlie, I love you, and I don't mean to pry, but please tell me what went wrong."

"She hasn't been feeling well. As you know, Micki has asthma, and she needs time to sort some things out."

Sort some things out? What did *that* mean? He was hurting. Yet he was still protecting her or some piece of himself that, after all these years, still remained terribly vulnerable.

"But you're twenty years older. What about 'for richer, for poorer, 'til death do us part'?" I asked.

"My age is part of the problem. The French say that the right age for a woman is half the man's age plus seven. That might be good for the French, but it didn't work out for me."

"Are you angry?"

His eyes started to tear ever so slightly behind his glasses. He reached behind his back into his right pocket for his perfectly starched handkerchief, which he unfolded in neat little squares. He blew into it, refolded the cloth, wiped his eyes, and placed it back in his pocket.

"She walked out on me. No one has ever done that

to me. I don't understand what I did. You know, sometimes I'm very direct with my words. I upset her. I don't mean to, and as soon as it's brought to my attention I always say, 'Honey, I'm sorry ... please forgive my wrong words.' This is one of my faults. I try to work on it, though at my age it's a little harder to fix things. You can't change a person's nature. I've always said that. This is my nature. But I really love her, and I want her back."

I had always loved Micki. She was easy to talk to, amenable to most of Papa Charlie's wishes, and patient. We knew it was sometimes difficult being married to a much older man, but that was an expectation before the marriage. I thought she and Papa Charlie were a wonderful couple. I asked if I might call her to talk.

"Of course," he said.

"Do you think you two can work it out?"

"I'm hopeful. Still, one never knows. Love is such a contradiction. Pragmatists fall for idealists. Swingers wind up with players. Nesters try to smother butterflies. If this weren't so serious I'd laugh about it."

"How do you stay so optimistic? If I were you I would be hiding under the sheets."

"Naturally, I'm not happy it's come to this. In the end there are only two outcomes: Micki and I get back together, or she decides against continuing our marriage—in which case, I'm stuck."

Micki chose not to reconcile. She divorced Papa Charlie several months later after thirteen years of marriage.

My grandfather was philosophical and made the best of the situation.

"Always be an optimist," he advised. "Remember: It wasn't *so* bad. Sometimes the suspense is worse than the ordeal."

Twenty-five

A Place Called Shalom

I started to ask Papa Charlie about death when he was in his eighties. Not because I was morbid; I was curious about his "relationship with God." Although Papa Charlie always believed certain things were expected of him, he also hoped for some kind of divine "reciprocation."

"What do you want from God?" I asked him.

"A long and healthy life. I hope He feels I'm deserving of it."

We were sitting in his office next to a portrait my mother had painted of him.

"Does it ever scare you ... dying, I mean?"

"No," he said briskly. But I wasn't exactly convinced. His exercise and diet regimens were so strictly adhered to; it must be because he was trying to defend himself against death. Or was it just to protect himself from aging badly?

"What do you think happens afterward?" I asked.

"I hope I will go to the Other Side and be able to look after the family and you as I always have." He leaned more comfortably into his chair. "I've watched after you every single day of your life, and I'll look after you every single day for the rest of your life from the Other Side. *And don't ever forget it.*"

"I know you will, Papa Charlie," I said softly. I paused for a minute and asked, "Do you believe in reincarnation?"

"No. I hope God allows me to continue in some form what I've done here."

"You mean like community service?"

He laughed. "Something like that."

"Have you ever felt the presence of your mother or father in all the years they've been gone? Or Beryl and Chaim, your brothers who died of diphtheria?"

"Beryl and Chaim I have thought of often because their deaths were a message to me that God intended me to live for a *reason*. I had two other brothers as well, whom you don't know anything about. Their names were . . ." He paused and made a face. "My memory is so bad. So many years have passed. Their names were Alexander and Benjamin. Your dad knew Benjamin. We called him Ellie. He died about fifty years ago. Alexander was a beautiful boy. He died in about 1920."

"Older or younger brothers?"

"Both were older. I was the eighth of my parents' nine children. Your Aunt Betty, whom you remember well, was the youngest." He became wistful. "I do think of my mother and father very often, but I don't know if I can say that I've felt their presence. I've never thought about it in that way, but it's a question worth pursuing."

"I would feel your presence."

"I would feel yours too, even if I didn't go to the Other Side."

"How?" I wondered.

"I don't know. I just feel in my bones that I would know about you, unless of course we really do just turn to dust."

"What happens if that in fact is the truth? That all we become is *dirt*?"

"Well, I guess it means we would have had a few

entertaining conversations that no one will know about. And the rest of it won't make any difference."

"I don't believe—or I won't believe—that we don't go somewhere from here."

"I agree with you," Papa Charlie said. "My God, my God, after a complex experience such as life, why would it just stop? Surely something must follow."

"I have to believe that. Otherwise death is too frightening."

"I believe I'm at peace with death. I don't look forward to it, but at my age I have to be realistic. How many more years can I have? I'm eighty-five now. Will God give me five years more? Ten? Less? I don't know."

"I need you to be here until you're a hundred," I said.

"I'm planning on it. But remember after I'm gone, God will guide you. Judaism will give you faith. And I will be watching."

Twenty-six

Every Age Has Its Beauty

*A*t ninety Papa Charlie was still alert and physically active. He adhered to his sixty-five-year-old regimen of calisthenics, followed by a deadly breakfast of grapefruit, hot water, hot milk, and goopy-tasting blackstrap molasses.

"I'm still walking, talking, golfing, swimming, and playing bridge. What else can one ask for?" Papa Charlie boasted. "I urged my good friend Justice William Brennan to do the same."

And his pal the Supreme Court justice Bill Brennan said of Papa Charlie, "He is an amazing example of vigor, an almost ageless man. Charlie is truly amazing."

Growing old was a positive, educational process for my grandfather. "I keep on learning new things," he insisted.

The family had a tradition of grand parties that began in earnest upon his seventieth birthday. Every fifth year thereafter, Papa Charlie gave himself a "milestone" celebration, which we all anticipated with enthusiasm.

At eighty-three he celebrated his second bar mitzvah; a third was scheduled during his ninety-sixth year.

"The older I become, the more satisfaction I seem to draw from life," he told me. "Some people my age believe there is a relationship between aging and maturity, that happiness is found in youth and naturally diminishes with age. Not so. No one is born happy."

He died in Palm Beach on December 30, 1995— coincidentally the same month in which I was born. He was with me at my beginning. I hope he felt my presence at his end.

Twenty-seven

Remembering Love

*P*apa Charlie always intended to live one hundred years, but six months after he turned ninety age began—slowly at first—to defy him. By the time he was ninety-three it had become the enemy.

His body was still youthful. His skin remained firm and virtually unlined. His limbs were nimble. He smelled good. Papa Charlie was still beautiful.

But his eyes no longer glowed with impishness and curiosity, and he was strangely silent. I often wondered what he was thinking—or if he was even able to think at all. Most of the time he appeared to have neither short- nor long-term memory. Was his mind, then, a black *blank?* Could he ponder *anything?*

The first time he didn't recognize me I could hardly

believe it. I had never planned for it, even though I knew his cerebral abilities were rapidly deteriorating.

Perhaps Papa Charlie knew more than I thought. Several months later, as I was about to enter the office elevator, I saw him and smiled. His eyes became young again. He pointed his rubber-ended cane at me and said enthusiastically, "I love him. I love him. I love him. I don't remember his name, but I love him."

Epilogue

"The journey doesn't end," he said. "You never know about dying, but death was nothing at all. You could say I went into another room for a while. At the moment it was happening I felt I was like rising steam. But now I am beside you again.

"I'll always be by your side."